THE ME I WAS WITH YOU

poems by

Jan Marin Tramontano

Finishing Line Press
Georgetown, Kentucky

THE ME I WAS WITH YOU

Copyright © 2021 by Jan Marin Tramontano
ISBN 978-1-64662-541-3 First Edition
All rights reserved under International and Pan-American Copyright Conventions. No part of this book may be reproduced in any manner whatsoever without written permission from the publisher, except in the case of brief quotations embodied in critical articles and reviews.

ACKNOWLEDGMENTS

Hibiscus, *Up the River*, Issue 1, 2013
The Art of Losing, *Up the River*, Issue 5, 2017
My Mother's Silk Scarf, *Up the River*, Issue 6, 2018

Publisher: Leah Huete de Maines
Editor: Christen Kincaid
Cover Art: Judith Prest
Author Photo: Karen Anglin
Cover Design: Elizabeth Maines McCleavy

Order online: www.finishinglinepress.com
       also available on amazon.com and at www.jantramontano.com

            Author inquiries and mail orders:
                  Finishing Line Press
                     PO Box 1626
              Georgetown, Kentucky 40324
                        USA

Table of Contents

Hibiscus 1

The Me I Was With You 3

The Art of Losing 4

    I. Cake Plates

    II. Scrapbooks

    III. Home

    IV. Garage Sale

    V. Artful Losing

Undertow 10

Lay Back the Darkness 12

A Last Night in the ICU 13

November Blues 14

Picture an Old-Fashioned Couple 15

At Paradise Nails 17

Breath 19

Solar Eclipse, Totality 20

Woman in a Poppy Dress 22

A Daily Ritual 24

My Mother's Silk Scarf 26

The Lilac outside My Window 27

Listen to the presences inside poems,
Let them take you where they will.
The Tent
Rumi

For Ron, our children and grandchildren
And all who have come before
And all who will follow

Hibiscus

It takes faith to coax a plant
from root to bloom. And
the gardener is a believer.

Working the soil, he replenishes
missing nutrients, creates a fertile bed
before a single shoot appears.

In his mind's eye, he sees the white
trumpet-shaped petals long before
the woody stalk begins its ascent.

All summer long, he tends cascading
wisteria, showy dinner plate dahlias
blasting out flugelhorns of color

patiently waiting for that time near
summer's end when the virginal blossom
with fuchsia center opens—

shimmers in the morning sunlight
only to close and drop at sunset.

All he invests in that single blossom
carries with it the weight and
significance of a solitary moment.

Next door, a long-awaited baby
was born. The years and months
leading to her birth was spent

envisioning a family of two
becoming three. But the dream
fulfilled lasted two short months

obliterated—
by an anonymous truck driver
who took this new mother in full bloom

plucked her from her own abundant garden
and dropped her hard to the ground.

Like the gardener who anticipates the
future we, too, need to believe in plans
despite uncertainty in the cycle of seasons.

The Me I Was With You

Crisp golden leaves drift
to the ground
swept away as you were.

Tuck Everlasting
boy with Autumn red mane
eyes bluest blue.

The me I was with you
also gone, but
through the many years
you linger, my companion

in orange blaze of sunset
in power of surging stream
I feel you in my fingertips—

> there—in gentle wind of summer
> in snappish smell of fall
> the taste of a snowflake

in your flutter to earth
you remain
fixed in time.

The Art of Losing

> *The art of losing isn't hard to master...so many things seem filled with intent to be lost that their loss is no disaster.*
> One Art / Elizabeth Bishop

I. Cake Plates

Pink roses on bone china, water glasses
rimmed with silver bands, crystal goblets
the polished silver tea service
all crowded onto the dining room table.

Once prized possessions, now burden.
My niece will take the china
my daughter the wine glasses
the rest cast off, become
quintessential garage sale.
My mother watches
rubbernecking an accident scene.

Let's pick four cake plates to keep.
She sneers, then softens
sees them as expectant wallflowers
hopeful they'll be chosen
and mutters, *don't forget who's the mother.*

*We'll keep the Aynsley bluebird and rose plate
you and Dad brought back from England.
But this one...* I shake my head. *Look
at the crackling on Dad's pineapple
upside down birthday plate.*

She rubs her finger over the chipped
edge as if to heal it, recalls how
she'd hold her breath, hope the
cherries nesting in sticky brown sugar
would release from the pan.
It goes into the discard pile.

I lift the hydrangea plate. We remember
Aunt Sarah's cinnamon crescents
taste buttery dough on our tongues.
I'll use it when you come over.
Take them. Throw them away. I don't care,
she grumbles, *crumb cake out of a box.*
and pushes the stack roughly toward me.

I choose four.

II. Scrapbooks

Musty boxes and plastic bins
stacked floor to ceiling
occupy a basement corner. I lug
two cardboard cartons upstairs
softened by years of dampness.

Bloated albums contain corsages, hair
ribbons, dance programs, yellowed
report cards, autographed photos.

Mom, I say, tell me every detail—
how you and grandma picked the fabric
and pattern for your dress,
the dance music, your date.

She nods. Both eager and reticent
to go back in time.

I lift the first album, wipe a dusty
film from the once creamy
cover. The pages are brittle.
Corsages crumble at the lightest touch.
Mom doesn't seem to notice.

Jerry Soless, she says. His name rolls
gently off her tongue, before the turn.
Now forgetful and distracted,
Jerry's betrayal with a best friend
still blisters.

She relives the deceit and
we gently place the ancient petals
the dance program and Jerry's picture
into a black plastic trash bag.

She hugs me when I leave
and whispers, *he never became half
the man your father is, you know.
And wasn't nearly as handsome.*

III. Home

Floorboards creak beneath unstable legs.
The bones of her home reveal hidden traps—
a loose tread on the stairs, uneven
thresholds, the bathtub growing deeper.

Water boils for tea, the kettle whistles
until its throat is dry. Transfixed,
she doesn't hear it.

The dining room rings with the voices
of her squabbling sisters, peevish through
old age, still clamoring to be Papa's favorite.

She remembers standing at the door
year of the Thanksgiving Day blizzard, watching
for late arrivals. Relief washes over her
once again as they trudge snow on the carpet.

Gazing out the dining room window
she sees the yard transformed, violinists play
Vivaldi on the back porch, her husband walks
their daughter towards the arched rhododendrons.

What she doesn't see are bald
brown patches in the lawn spreading
like liver spots, the list of the maple
her husband planted when they first moved in
the splintered swing
dangling from a dead branch.

She snaps back.

Now, she is the one swinging in the wind
and the breeze is no longer gentle.
Weary, she paces from one room to another
unwilling to imagine strangers inside her walls.

IV. Garage Sale

A loveseat, scratched nightstands
beds covered with crocheted afghans—
all displayed on the front lawn.
She walks into the house to see
if what her children agreed
she could keep is still there.
It is.

Back outside, she walks around
tables, dishes accumulated
through Green Stamps
lie amidst a mix of flatware.
She fingers a towel, traces
the rim of a china plate.

Neighbors sit on her husband's
recliner, strangers lie on the
couch her son brought to college
a teenage girl admires herself
in her makeup mirror.

Rather than strangers picking
through her things like rotting carcass,
she hopes a truck will pull up
take the contents of her life whole.

She will smile and tell them
to be careful of the short leg
on the dining room chair, the way
to prop up the glass shelf in the cabinet.

The dream moment disappears and
she watches as the tangible memories
of her once ago life disappear
into unknown hands and her children fill
an old cigar box with dollars and coins.

V. Artful Losing

Her children don't notice
loss burrowing into every pore.

They plow ahead, clear the field
for new homesteaders

who won't realize their seedlings will be
full grown before they know it.

Time is an erratic thief, she will warn them.
Don't bother to lock your doors. It finds its way in.

The art of losing isn't hard to master—
> keys, names, voices of old friends,
> her mother's face.

She will become the person who believes:
> *so many things seem filled with the intent*
> *to be lost that their loss is no disaster.*

Undertow

If I close my eyes
I can still feel
the smoothness
of the weathered
boards beneath my feet
feel the caress
of silky sand
between my toes
hear
crashing breakers.
Daddy would lift
me high over
white-capped waves
build intricate castles
intent
as any child
only to lose interest
and walk away.

At home
he'd pull me
in a wagon
simulate the vroom
of a racecar
and then,
stop abruptly
a sudden pull
into undertow
his erratic moods
a volley
between
playful and peeved.

Now in senior housing
Daddy pulls
a battered wagon

of Styrofoam boxes—
soup and salad
a gravied entrée
cream pie.
Hooking his foot
on the wheel,
he trips. Splayed
on the carpet,
flattened containers

pool around him
in a humiliating river.

I'd help him
into that wagon
speed down
the long hallways
away from the ruins,
listen for his shout
faster, go faster.

Wait—
for his elusive
glint of smile
the one
beneath the dark
the one
I see coming
toward me
in the whistling waves.

Lay Back the Darkness
After Edward Hirsch

Vast, lonely canvas of night
Lay back the darkness for my father.

Neither rising moon nor shimmering
stars offer consolation—

He closes his eyes against the black,
vaults back into battle.

No longer the young boy digging trenches
to avoid flying bullets, he is now General.

Combatant to the last possible battle
he staves off the army of malignant intruders.

Surrounding them with a battalion
armed with poison arrows,

he insists his riverbeds be widened
to feed their narrow streams.

With pummeled body,
his will remains unscarred.

Vast lonely canvas of night until later.
Lay back the darkness for my father.

A Last Night In The ICU

As my father lay dying
the family surrounds his bed
the decision made to stop

treatment, his pain blunted
the atmosphere becomes upbeat
my perpetually frowning sister

smiles, signals the hospitable nurse
to bring a tray—coffee, tea, water, pastry
my father, pleasantly drugged

replays family fables
pauses, demands kisses
from my flustered, confused mother

the rabbi stops by mumbles a quick
prayer, delighted in the unexpected levity.
As baffled as my mother

I watch the incongruous scene
every bit the outsider, watch
these actors deliver their lines

a familiar script, dubbed
in a foreign language.

November Blues

Once November's stinging air
colorless palette and leafless trees
served as backdrop for
my own fading pallor.

But like the birds
eagerly flying south
I too migrated away
from skies layered gray.

I now live in palm tree land
among shades of orange and pink,
air refreshingly cool, dissipating
the thickness of summer.

Yet sense memories collide.

In autumn myself
now heading for winter
I live among the forever hopefuls,
*blue zoners** who dance, walk and, jog
to halt seasonal headwinds.

Perhaps, if I didn't have
the fresh memory
of the hollow sound of dirt
thudding on my father's casket

I could more easily absorb
the gentler sensation
of tropical breezes
nudging me to look upward
into the blue.

*The Blue Zone Project supports the lifestyles and environments embraced by the world's longest-lived people.

Picture An Old-Fashioned Couple

bride and groom atop a wedding cake
The man—stocky with wavy black hair
and thick mustache. The woman—
slender, with tawny hair twisted into a
bun held by a single pin.

A far-flung image for Holocaust survivors
but that is how I saw them.
Although a short distance from my house to theirs,
it was a border crossing.

They lived in space crowded with heavy
velvet furniture covered with
brocade scarves, beneath a wall
of unsmiling sepia-toned portraits,
a shelf lined with yellow
foul smelling candles, lit daily.

Books and more books
piled haphazardly
on tables, chairs, the floor,
in English, Russian, Polish, Yiddish.

Muted opera played on
an old phonograph.

In her 1950s kitchen, Ruth served
hot tea in glasses, sugar cube held
between their teeth. They drank
from the steaming glasses as if ice water.
Talked of books, politics, history. No chitchat,
no gossip. Derisive of the shallow
Americans they were forced to live among.

Ruth, a vibrant storyteller described her life *before*.
The Warsaw she loved.
Before.
The family life she had.
Before
The melodious language she spoke.
Before

And then, there was
After.
Kristallnacht, sucking them into hell.
After.
Unspeakable deeds committed for survival.
After.
Total loss:
Country.
Home.
Profession.
Son.

I remember the details of that long-ago afternoon—
the smells from old books and candles.
Porcelain dolls standing on the piano,
their marble eyes frozen in surprise,
children who would never die.

At Paradise Nails

I sit in a pedicure chair next
to a tall man with a deeply creased,
acned face. Too big for the chair,
he slouches.

On his left leg is a tattoo with
a soaring eagle seared by a long
white scar. Semper Fi
peeks out of his open shirt.

An Asian face on his muscled arm
reminds me of the renamed Tiffany
Katelyn and Jenny at Paradise Nails

who treat clients as an anonymous
array of hands and feet and legs,
their English business only—
what need, pick color, water too hot?

I wonder about the Vietnamese banter
sometimes brisk, but often playful
as they sand dead skin from the soles of feet
and clip cuticles and twirl steaming towels.

An oddity here, I never would have
imagined this aging marine as someone
who would come into this chiefly
female world of soak and scrape

and swirling water, but I notice him
leaning in to listen and I wonder
if he understands them until
I hear an almost imperceptible sigh

when the impervious Tiffany squirts
lemongrass and orange lotion onto his legs
and begins the deep massage, her touch
transports him—

his bulky body changes shape
as he melts into the chair
closes his eyes and a roguish smile
brightens his face.

Breath

I lay awake at night
snug, under a pile of
silken blankets.

My husband
who says he never sleeps
snores lightly.

I am soothed
by the whistle of his
inhale, then exhale.

A few days later
I stand with him
at his mother's bedside.

We listen to the labor
of her breath. Its shallowness
followed by a skip, then hiccup.

Anxious for her next breath
we realize we hold ours,
until there is silence.

Solar Eclipse, Totality

The residents buzz
excited
about the solar eclipse
energy surging
from one
resident to the next
in the ordinarily
static assisted living lobby.

Everyone talks at once
What is it? Where is it?
When can I see it?
Sylvia demands, *What will I see?*
Herb warns, *Watch your eyes!*
Gladys worries, *Where are your dark glasses?*

Pushing their walkers
towards the TV in the lobby
most residents don't understand
what the fuss is about
but any diversion from Monday
afternoon bingo is welcome.

My mother has no idea
what an eclipse is
but is cheered by the excitement
whirling around her.
She rifles through her purse
this time with a real mission—
finding her sunglasses.

Arnold, who sits next
to her at dinner told her
she must wear them if she
goes outside or she'll go blind.
She nervously watches him
hobble out, sunglasses in hand
ready to see something magical
in an ordinary blue-sky summer day.

It first occurred to me that afternoon
that my mother embodies
that solar eclipse—
sunlit chatter, suddenly darkened,
an immediate plummet
into a singular world.

At the moment the world waits
to see totality, I want my world
to normalize.
Let the darkness
slowly pass over the sun
this one time
and then forever return
light and darkness
to their rightful places.

Woman in a Poppy Dress

I walk to the wine bar, happy
in my new sundress
bright as a poppy field.

An old man with chop stick
legs, feet cushioned in sturdy
soles, pushes a walker
careful to avoid missteps.

Not wanting to think about
what may lie ahead, I shift
my attention to children
running down the street.

A small blonde girl in pink ruffles
chases her bigger brother. Neat and fresh
pressed, they remind me of my girls,
one always skipping ahead of the other
daring to be caught.

I smile, think I see them just up ahead
racing toward the ice cream shop
I want to call out to them, tell them
to slow down, I can't keep up
in my new strappy sandals.

For a moment, I'm back in time
until I look down at my brightly
colored toes bent this way and that
brittle twigs on a mottled branch.

I look away from my feet
from my reflection
in the shop window
from any vestige
of the aging me.

Let that be for now—
Instead, I sashay down the street
like I once did, owning that dress
brimming with poppies
        back to when
I was the young bride,
        then the young mother,
        then the woman not stopped
for directions but for a closer look.

Daily Ritual

It's 4:30.

I know it without looking at a clock
a daily ritual

time for my mother's call
I hear the silence and hold the space

often irritated by the daily calls
I thought them intrusive, annoying

although she was a dramatic storyteller
with tasty gossip to amuse me

and yet now, they are no more

now, I make the call
not at 4:30

but through the day
the phone rings once, twice

six, ten, fifteen times
sometimes nursing home staff answers
oftentimes not

sometimes my mother will talk
sometimes she'll drop the phone

sometimes she'll tell a fabulist story
about police and courtrooms

now she is in random episodes of
Law and Order we loved to watch

her ropes are frayed past mending
yet I long to braid the vibrancy back to life

sometimes our 4:30 calls still happen
I'll imagine Mom reach

for the wall phone in her kitchen
while she smooths her perfect blonde hair

I strain when I hear a Sinatra song playing
the whir of an old bonnet hair dryer

the silence on the other end of the phone
noisy with memory.

My Mother's Silk Scarf

I have a scarlet silk scarf that
smells like my mother.
Not sweet like *Evening in Paris*
nor the cloying flowers of
Chloe, and certainly not
the confident here-I-am *Chanel*.

She was not the *Chanel* type.
More fresh scrubbed girl
next door, bathed in talcum powder.
The way I always imagined
Katharine Hepburn might smell.

Now, my mother doesn't
remember this scarf, worn only on
Saturday date night with my father.
Nor will she remember what
perfume she wore. Sometimes
she doesn't even remember me.

I cover my face with its silky softness
see her squeeze her atomizer
a puff drifts in its folds
she smiles as my father
takes her hand
twirls her, light and free
to *Moonglow*.

The Lilac Outside My Window

cold seeps through down jackets
and caulked windows
winter—

late sunrise, early sunset
a blanket of gloom falls
on ground frozen brown

but stirrings of life still thrive—
cardinals and nuthatches pick at seed
acrobatic squirrels swing on feeders

the graceful arched limbs
of a lilac bush outside my window
remind me of the sweet smell of future

when my daughters were small
they would bring me a breakfast tray
on Mother's Day morning

coffee and cinnamon toast
with sprigs from that lilac
and sticky jelly kisses.

Jan Marin Tramontano is a poet and novelist. Her books include: three poetry chapbooks, *Floating Islands, A Woman Sitting in a Café and Other Poems of Paris* and *Paternal Nocturne*, two novels, *What Love Becomes* and *Standing on the Corner of Lost and Found*, and her father's memoir, *I am a Fortunate Man*. Her poems also appear in her poetry collective's anthologies, *Java Wednesdays*. and *Peer Glass Review*.

Jan's short stories, poetry and novel excerpts have been published in numerous literary journals, magazines, and newspapers including *Adelaide Literary Magazine, AOIS 21, Up the River, Poets Canvas, Chronogram, Women's Synergy, Knock, The DuPage Valley Review, Moms Literary Review, New Verse News* and *Byline*. Her work also appears in *Ophelia's Mom* and *Surviving Ophelia*. In addition, her poems have won several poetry contests including *Poets & Writers*.

Jan holds a BA in Sociology from Boston University and an MA from the University at Albany in Communications. She has participated in writing workshops throughout the country including the New York State Writers Institute, Florida Gulf Coast University's Renaissance Academy's Writers Collaborative, the Iowa Summer Writers Festival, a summer writing workshop at Mabel Dodge Luhan House in Taos, New Mexico, the International Women's Writing Guild, and the Poetry Forge workshop series.

After a long career in public health, Ms. Tramontano turned to her first love and worked as an independent writing consultant offering research, writing, and editing services to a wide array of clients.

A lifelong resident of upstate New York, Jan was a longtime member of the Hudson Valley Writers Guild and served on the board, as program chair, and contest administrator. She also was very active in the spoken word community and was honored with many featured poet appearances throughout the region. She now lives with her husband in Naples, Florida.

www.ingramcontent.com/pod-product-compliance
Lightning Source LLC
LaVergne TN
LVHW041513070426
835507LV00012B/1552